Predators Welcome

GW01451724

"Coursing through a cauterized national-cultural landscape, transmogrifying spent notions of Self, The Other, and many a vaunted We, Krieger's dionysian fury—Krieger at the mic—is a riveting art form to behold. Gaining devotees by the day (I am one of those Kriegies), her poetics evinces a strength of intellect and flow of feeling that's singular in intensity. In *Predators Welcome*, we delight in the dismantling of All-American Redemptory Poetics (the hegemon of our times) through a nimble dialectics of Body & Alt-Body, Pain & Infra-Pleasure. Dylan Krieger is not a this-or-that brand of poet, but an *accelerant* to poetry itself."

—Rodrigo Toscano, author of *The Cut Point* (Counterpath) and *Collapsible Poetics Theater* (Fence Books, Winner of the National Poetry Series)

Predators Welcome

Dylan Krieger

LIMIT ZERO Publications
Portland, Oregon

LIMIT ZERO

PUBLICATIONS

This book is published by LIMIT ZERO Publications
www.LMTzero.com

Cover Design by Joel Amat Güell
joelamatguell.com

Interior Design by Gigi Little
gigilittle.com

Published in the United States of America
ISBN 978-1-938753-48-0

Contents

PREDATORS WELCOME

"All these hunters who are shrieking now,
oh, do they speak for us?"

—Leonard Cohen
"Stories of the Street"

FOR THE WASHABLE TATTOO ATOP A PERMANENT SCAR

whether a fire, cancer
slip of the wrist with a razor in the shower

the only evidence left is a pale sheen
of fingerprintless disbelief

in skin rebuilt, fine lines flattened
into unidentifiable cropland gone fallow

black thumb all through summer
and the soil spits blood back

but look: there is a painted piece of paper
that obviously wants to cover the world up

and it's whatever color you want it to be, baby
golden, lavender, ruby

little fistful of familiar confetti-ing over
a headstone like it's new year's in hell

to think: the attention welcome for once
and stuffed with wet petals

when they fall off we're different
crystalline coats fully saturated

weighted down with old gods in the pockets
to keep from floating away

i wish anyone could say *reconstructive* and mean it
but they're always sort of smirking

fine that the stitches stay in
fine that the willows bend over just to fuck us

if not the tumors, contusions
what would we cover in tinsel and expensive juices

these are the landmarks that tell extinction
it's moving in the right direction

unhook the horror from the headwound and be honest:
even the lily's better gilded

ALL THE MICE MULTIPLYING INSIDE THE PROMISE I MADE YOU

nature's favorite flavor of relationship is neglect

under the fabric, squirming soft

pinning a silver medal to a beachhead

the waves say, *stop murdering*   *allow me*

so we let them, but then it gets so quiet

we can hear the last analogue clock stop

and the violence settles instead

in our jaw bones, dry needled to ribbons

for this body, torture is simple:

a flick of the absentminded nerve ending

gentlest caress hemmed in by pin cushions

if this is an interrogation

tearful echo in the confessional

whistle where one tooth didn't chip

race you to the end of this story and in the next

maybe happiness won't matter, rats spottable a mile off

while there are no witnesses, open your trench coat

to the elements: let's see the swarm

everyone warned of, fornicating like a work of art

STAY LUCID IN THE DREAM LONG ENOUGH TO MAKE OUT WITH YOUR MONSTERS

paper roses of prison pinned to my tiny
childhood bedroom i remember
when friends looked like cooked flies
on mom's windshield 9 o'clock sharp
nighttime in local county lockup where mikey's window
faced the alley and somehow beyond logic
we enlisted our parents to be in on it
back and forth block to block the west side unkillable
small town out of a storybook too shitty to be published
wishes are the things delicately affixed with scotch tape
to the walls of cells never entered too scared
but i was there out back countless drive-bys
riding shotgun into darkness headlights off
i read the letters aloud said *yes* to the charges
dressed up for a court date before i could vote
we don't even talk now but i heard hard time happened
i hope it's over but then again what do i know
landlocked civilian propaganda handed down
over and over *don't stay sore for the sake of it*
the only maxim that matters in anger
what the flowers were oozing this whole time anyway
come home one day and find the robin's eggs
broke open and what is there to say about the world
aboutfaced   about the screaming
turned to laughing   about the change?

IF ALL MY EXISTENTIAL REVERIES COME TRUE
AND I RETURN AS MOLTEN GOO

i would like to be surprising like the earth's
core coming up for air

oh wait they call that a volcano
oh wait they call that

world war whatever the fuck
do you remember the last time a stomach

cradled all civilization at once
long enough to vomit it back up

this is the way it always works
witless ocean-like lockjaw

nothing so violent as my masseter
against itself so do your worst

what does hell have to lose? what are
all these ambulances even here for?

a living medical anomaly
never-before-seen human suit removal

say it like you will to the police
i am pure practice for something

spotlight-come-later in the
interrogation chamber

i am the front lawn yawning open
so wide you'll never count the teeth

THE GHOST OF CORPORATE FUTURE LOOKS LOST

remember less responsibility?
smaller office, frilly abdomen
in love with a lot of loose ghosts

i laugh hardest when people act sure of things
like interest rates, outdated copyright law
the banking habits of the rich and famous

or even just your average adult
30-year mortgage out of money market
$1,000 for a cat funeral, poorly attended

i went *boo!* and the whole future got spooked
scurried into the basement, back claws a-clatter
how's that for a promotion? to scare shitless

the witchlord himself, to open up the heart
mid-attack, to look down
at dirt disturbed, even the buried

don't stay in one place here
even the teeth do not keep
and think of all the flesh they've chewed through

all the while grinding into oblivion
rendering powerless until rendered powerless
over and over the predator—   reassembles

I KNOW I FUCKED THE DEVIL LAST NIGHT BUT THE REST IS SOLID BLACKOUT

on nights he catches me at home
we sit opposite each other, sipping
from the same drugged cocktail

lose a little time swallowing body parts
i find a used condom in the trash
the day after, a detective of

my own distorted timeline
fresh nightmare spread out
on the pillow like milk

i wish i'd been awake
to hear his hiss through clenched teeth
throat-sicing fists unflinching

circle by circle, we make it through the inferno
and then keep punching blind
to the slideshow, i don't believe in *souls*

i don't believe in *beyond help*
but i believe in the atrocity that happens
between us and everyone it's getting off

in the afterlife we call the internet
where we're unearthed in perpetuity
safely watched

STRATEGIC EGO STROKING ON THE NOT-TOO-DISTANT NEW YORK HORIZON

covert cocktails in the cabin from louis armstrong

to laguardia, yes, i have traveled 1,000 miles

a whole new species of booty call

sucking down cold showers, semblance of charlotte

north carolina disappearing into rearview tarmac

we wish sometimes the whirlwind might

turn overnight into a life

we'd wake up so in love with last call's haul

we'd stop searching at all

but that's not quite the river i cross

into brooklyn from queens

i believe in the boogeyman and not much else

i believe and then the opposite happens

i believe in the descent and never know until the splat

HE LEFT A HAND-SHAPED BRUISE RIGHT WHERE THE HEART WOULD BE IF I WERE HUMAN

and then the golden room goes dark
the sodium orange moon swells until it busts

i candy flip for the first time on the staten island ferry
and later you put all your weight on me

not passively, but like you push a car, concentrated
on the collapsible curve of my breastbone

the depth that flesh bends before hemorrhage
when the trains pass we go silent together

just long enough to remember other methods
of communicating, sprockets and microchips

sex and electrodes, the expansion of your pupil
at a specific elevation over the east river

play me like an out-of-tune piano on the back
of a pickup truck covered in christmas lights

i am nothing but a long series of failures
to jump the turnstiles before puking

down the subway platform you tell me
the life stories of other vermin as if they matter now

that you're the animal burrowing fastest into power
now that the city keeps my cicada wings on display

for all to break, and you let it, just to hear
the sound i make, the anti-language

past surrender
the impossible rape

YET ANOTHER UNSUCCESSFUL ATTEMPT TO BREAK UP WITH MYSELF

whiplash, the only reliable lover left
who is this night bird of apostrophe
i hush endlessly with my intimate sickness?

why write the very worst thing down?
because the devouring happens
with or without the sound of the alarum

my doctor answers, plugging one of my tentacles
back into the worldwide wolf cry
where i shouldn't but can't help

recognizing myself
as every eye's
last flash

SOMETIMES THE SADNESS SITS CLOSER TO THE SURFACE

new travelog plan where i send you weirdly regional
nudes from airbnb bathrooms across the country
and you don't respond

i need an industrial-strength dose of *boy, bye*
to rise up from the mud, i need the tall tower of libido
to topple longways with utmost friction and thickness

i need a costco-sized cock and no permission from god
to make a robot blush
dance over detonated glass

echolocate the will to live from the edge of the pit
we remember scraping by on bitter berries
but why   but what

directionless headwinds do we defy each morning
by leaving a little more of ourselves
dead in the bottle to pickle

if i am supposed to know the ending by now
we're in trouble, if i am supposed to keep you
locked up like a bloodhound in my underwear

the potion is working, the dark woods are barking
you are taking out your rifle and pointing it
straight at the sun

EVERY MORNING FOR BREAKFAST I GOOGLE MY WORST FEAR AND IT'S DELICIOUS

on a scale from tundra to louisiana
it's like temperate michigan march
snowdrifts receding from the lawn
chance of me falling in love when i fuck

if the rain came down right now
would it freeze midair or not
do you know anything about me yet
besides the innards turned velvet

mad habits pumping
rhythm of addiction pinned
as tight as fluids can manage
you tell me about your older brothers

but they, too, could be anyone
smeared faces on the canvas
gooey stains across the mattress
imagine what we'd have to lose

to be strangers again: not much
there are methods of making magnetic attraction
way scarier, says summer to the other seasons
and they listen so long they stop talking at all

until one day the water wakes up steam
until the heat levitating is the only god that speaks

THE PRESENT MOMENT CUDDLES UP TO EXISTENCE AND NOTHINGNESS WITHOUT PREFERENCE

the universe is a museum of chilly feelings
caught by glass, defined by the gaps
i forget to rotate the house plants for months
and after, they're permanent-bent
in centripetal window reach
such is the photosynthetic calling we're born into
above the kitchen sink, with our long stems hung down
for the cat to bat at
and believe it or not, i carry this whole ecological
disaster around with me
buckle it in for road trips, feed it its vitamins
read it its horoscopes
the hope is that the black fog will raise us up with it
and let us drop
the hope is that we're onto something when we touch
and bake like beach grass in sun
i want to be pummeled with the subtropical
marriage proposals of star radiation
so hard that i don't have to lift a single branch
i want to watch you like a chemtrail
snaking down the skyline
an invasive dust the rest of us cannot cough out

ALL RANSOM NOTES ARE SECRETLY ABOUT POUGHKEEPSIE AND ROTTEN MEAT

tell me about the last time you reunited with fire
a jet engine explodes behind the catskills
as we point and gawk like tourists, same setting
we met in at 18—train upstate, buses cross-country
your hometown, parents' empty house, vodka and
pineapple on the back deck until the treeline freaks out
when i cry, men short-circuit in the ratchetest fashion
and stick me on the soonest transport back to the city
no place to stay in manhattan but borrowed rooftops
sticky park benches, talking my best friend off the ledge
of revenge when even the flight log is spelled wrong but
then he mentions the meat market with its dried hooves
infinity of fluorescent lights echoing flatfish eyes
anatomy of snail-mail magazine clippings sponged shut
with rubber gloves, rerouted through major metropolises
on both coasts, undustable for prints, anonymous grids
cornering the country into smoke-filled tongue kiss
and at the height of so-called passion, the veil just rips
and rips and rips, and the heap of threads you left
to scatter knows exactly where you live

KILL THE HYMEN SAVE YOURSELF

aside from the wildfires
what's so new about a world ordered
by random pinpricks of damage

i laugh in barbie's face when it breaks
and ask my mother to explain
in terms of diagrammed britannica

something tangible to wipe the glisten
of my own rain off the page as i tower
high above the fear of change

because it's already happened
because i am open now for the bats
to fly into, to make their roost, to stay

DON'T WORRY, I HAVE NOT YET MASHED YOU INTO THE GROWING JELLO MOLD OF MEN WHO HAVE DISAPPOINTED ME

getting the feelings fucked out
on a spare mattress by the irish channel

i still think of your silent film sidebar
mountains of concrete that keep us

far apart spinning tops of stimulants
diluted by dark liquor

i'm a little lost without the rancid scent
of meaning something to anyone

and it's embarrassing on a daily basis
i walk like the restaurant's a runway

in case the eye-catch of a stranger
is what i'm waiting for—this isn't desperation

i'm named after the seabird who eats you only halfway
and i live up to it, with my fangs bared at the bottom

of the lake i call your name and you come running
i call your name and you evaporate

meet me at the dry well
underbelly of the bridge

at the end of the credits
when we're the only ones left listening

MY GENOME NEEDED A PROOFREADER SO THAT'S EXACTLY WHAT I'LL BE

i intend to get caught, not like a disease
but like a misprint
mark me red hot in alphanumerical shorthand

line-edit the log of the living as closely as possible
at the cellular level
leave it to the mitochondria to mutiny or else ruthlessly

work your fingernails into the wasp's nest made
manifest: direction in which all ashes scatter
reduced to four letters

we never decided this
born into it is an understatement
almost every preposition applies: *through, on, with, at*

i'm here and then i'm collection of whatnot
acid spirals expertly mimicking staircases from the 14th
century—beyond sentience

there is a science to feeling safe
only once
and then trying to recreate it for the rest of your life

there is a science to maiming what you can of what's left
and then there is the soft spot
where it was snowing

at the center of the sod farm and nowhere else
when you carried me back to the car that night
and said, *no one will ever believe us but ourselves*

ONE PERSON'S EMPTY PACK OF MARLBORO REDS IS ANOTHER'S TALISMAN OF TRANSPORT INTO PAST AND FUTURE LIVES

for longer than speaking terms
the empties stayed right where you left them

under the passenger's seat
enacting the impossibility of touch

what exactly we lack is lost on us
half the time, the last three-ringed

circus of circumstance
smoked down to the filter

crushed together into the car carpet
we witnessed the side-by-side

primordial origami, folded into each other
plastered wet leaves to the promise

compost represents: to reincarnate romance
between inanimate objects, to flatten into mulch

unmindful, yes, by definition—
the collection, changed, exchanged

dropping all it cannot carry
in its miracle wake

AUTOPSY REVEALS LASTING MARRIAGES MOSTLY COMPOSED OF SHARP METAL IN A THEORETICAL VACUUM

i am a longitudinal experiment in elopement
and the results are what you might call
good on paper, as in, they're still together

i've never been arrested, listened in class
well enough to welcome into my bloodstream
the great canonical misogynists of history

what a setback success is, you have to
unlearn everything, and then keep it
hanging around your house like an antibody

it's touch-and-go with me and weddings
forget red-tinted glasses, even with a pile of full-blown
roses up over my head, my mother comes

wandering through sometimes with her two black eyes
the kind you might separate over, but not divorce
that's what i absorbed, looming large above

the lesson planners, about what bad men deserve
when the window shoppers point and huff
embarrassed not by what he's done

but by the gall of this girl
to raise her face above the document
to show it off

THE WALKING TALKING AMERICAN CRISIS THAT IS MY IMMEDIATE FAMILY

dad's bad eyes helped him dodge nam

and mom's slipped disc brought vicodin

ripe for the swiping

this is how we mythologize a boon

out of the body's chaos

all the *disowned* and then not disowned

cut off and then tacked back on

the fucking yo-yo of some people's best attempt

at love, my god

and i am one of them: same nose

born as warm as i would get

what comes next is a decades-long

religious slur

bubbling in the throats of intoxicated caretakers

earlier iterations of sister stoned to death, over and over

i remember nothing

and i remember it so well that it scares everyone

convinced the kids weren't watching

they tied our wrists to a coke balloon

and walked back to the block party

sure it would hover there forever

shading our hair, tinting our skin

a bitter golden lived in ever since, together

BACK WHEN MEN RETURNED MY CALLS FOR REASONS OTHER THAN NOTES ON THEIR MANUSCRIPTS

there was a firsthand survey conducted on
straddle-height countertops
mom & pop motels so far down I-80
the midwest turns desert
there were gumball machines full of engagement rings
and we bought them all
married someone different on every finger
broke our vows with direct sunlight and a
magnifying glass atop a rock formation
teeth sunk so deep we had to leave them
under the scabs like shrapnel
car broke down, accounts empty, kicking college
like a tin can down a hill too steep to catch it
and by the time we made it to the bottom
the field was barren, the banks were flooded
in my knapsack i still keep stacks of love letters
old photos, dried flowers
and take them out once in a while
to whisper, *hush now, i get it*
enough with the exposition

I DREAMED A COMPLETE, POINTLESS SUNRISE OVER OSCEOLA, INDIANA

regurgitated landscape, back down the gullet
worm by worm: *homesick* isn't the hunger but
the filled-to-the-gills-with-it
someone else's memories of 8th grade
goth kid white supremacists
too early to say whether his face would stick that way
but late enough in the summer, there's almost
no escape, *maze* is a pun you can't run from
every gradient of sky-change looks like doomsday
ten-headed chemical, four corporate horsemen
after armageddon, my first love found me on an
airstrip middle of nowhere farms and graveyards
and we watched the moon intricately seam-rip
itself out of existence, sat back at such a distance
from the climax, in the midwest
we have hours to figure out how to cheers a shared beer
in the bed of the pickup, all morning to excruciate over
the colors of the mushroom, delicious or poisonous
we have as long as it takes
for the cloud-stems to reach us
drug store cigar break on the sidewalk
until the crock pot shuts off automatically
full week of snowmelt saved in cisterns
for us to sip from in our sleep

YES, BLACK HOLE, I TOO AM AN ALL-DEVOURING PERVERSION OF STARLIGHT COLLAPSED INTO A SINGLE GRAVITATIONAL POINT

at the center of the galaxy, fight me
with an absolute forest

invisible blizzard—some people want
to be annihilated

orbiting organisms on a large enough
scale can stop breathing

yet mete out such pressure we wonder
what hell could erupt like real life

where all solar systems secretly worship
at the altar of darkness

and i swallow every sweet thing
i want to say via satellite

because there is only room for so much
gut-wrench in each bottle

so i save it up and tell the story
of the train tracks, river-bloated body

bloody knife in a leaf pile
perfectly raked by the playground that day

how lonely the world looks
from right goddamn here

under the streetlamp of infinite flicker
fuck space

THE HEADLONG BILDUNGSROMAN OF ADDICTION TELLS ITS STORY OUT OF ORDER

at the block party, squashed under an ashtray
i follow my mother underground
in chubby second-grade braids

the basement ties its arm, nods off
i say i'm sorry to every junkie
for interrupting

i say nothing when grown men hit on my sister
but we memorize bright makeup
as what marks a moving target

new tendrils of terror in the phrase
dad loved: *grownup stuff*, door slammed
until the very faculty of speech dropped out

no one else knew the name of their parents'
dealer's girlfriend, dripping black bandeau
boob sweat at the concert of astonishment

but it's okay, i felt like an undercover angel
fly on the wall of so much strange
shrinking myself as small as possible

on the drive home from chicago
the lights looked different than before
not only neon of nightfall along the pier

ferris wheel flashing
smell of dead fish washed ashore
but what it meant: to touch the bottom and come back

to the home of the terrified and the land of the bored

AMIDST GLOBAL CATACLYSM MY RETIREMENT PLAN IS TO LEAVE THIS OLD WALLET AND A LITTLE WEED IN A WELL-LOVED POCKET FOR LATER

on vacation you say there is a plan to eradicate
the invasive species on this island before it gets
as overrun as the mainland and i wonder about
the logic of propping up interventionism with
more interventionism—the first sequel to the
indigenous original was scary enough as it is
don't you think? pocketed seedpod full of insect
eggs on the plane back to the states where
come to think of it, every sprig of tenderness
i spring from is non-native
prettiest red blooms exotically toxic
it's not that the transplants carry some canker
but like me their breed needs a natural predator
someone to be dangled by, recklessly, over fire
something to run from or else become part of
the moment of capture should crackle forever
indefinite delay between chase and digestion
where we are so close you're almost inside but
not quite and i don't dare budge from the incision
site with its extravagant unstable formula
for human flight—i don't imagine any other ending
i don't imagine i survive

If You Were Raised by the Same Wolves I Was

if you were raised by the same wolves i was

you know what it's like
to break bad news to the universe

little limbs poised
to clench thorns between paw pads

we stare at the sky like
it might gush blood any moment

a neat way to explain
where it all went the day of the crash

legs only half attached
you want me to be talking about something else

a housefly, a fire ant, but too bad
the miniscule is only preferable because you can't hear

the filaments tearing into various useless necklaces
the police could care less

the childlike negligence of
casually stomping whole colonies calms us

if we spring from the same progenerating
predators, welcome

to the thirst for flesh you'll never conquer
absolutely nothing happens for a reason

unless you just mean brute causation
like once the wolves

impregnated the angels
this car wreck was already waiting

at the edge of existence
deep breathing for its curtain entrance

to be nervous now is pointless, darling
go ahead: i'll do the driving, you reinvent the dead

if you were raised by the same wolves i was

whisper to me between scenes: what'd i miss?
i left the movie of our lives playing
while i was in the bathroom
i touched the coldest river to my hot hot wound
and didn't flinch
imaginary things matter
in the city of constant performance
so we drive south across the state line
go try dying on a mountain
stage a photo op with a desert rock
and wonder where *fake* comes from
ex nihilo adornment of the so-called natural order
rolled over to bake in the sun like a turtle
i show you portrait mode on the new iphone and
we both guffaw at the canyon blurred flat
peer underneath our ragged fingernails and
chew the sand out
sew our exhaustion into a butterfly net
dripping the romance it can't catch
but oh well
whosoever parachutes first off these cliffs wins
whosoever changes channels just by blinking
well, we're all waiting
with our tongues against your inseam
open or closed, it makes no difference—
we're breaking in

if you were raised by the same wolves i was

a strong accent makes you sound like
an android by comparison
loose bolts born of television news
to mimic men from nowhere

no matter what the wishing well is selling, i can dig
through the closets of skeletons and find better
for so cheap it's nothing, because coincidentally
as wet flyover trash myself, i am so cheap i'm nothing

and i tell the stranger on the street corner
that's what midwesterners have going for them:
the awareness of falling square beneath the boot-stomp
and not trying to stop it, decorating the tiny dome

between heel and toe as their own
coastless keepsake, settling in for another snowstorm
to escape is a long con and we're not fooling anyone
so we stay, perfectly afraid and dew-drenched

in our hospital bracelets, standing stock-still
scarecrow-style in never-photographed farmland
and the scavengers manage
to fly in through our sleeve-holes

but little do they imagine
we are not even human
little can their wings fathom
the fruit orchard already eaten 'til barren

the future turned lethal
by the skin of its systems
and all the signet rings of lesser gods outstretched
who wins best kisser?

if you were raised by the same wolves i was

you are sprucing yourself up for the end of the world
feeling weirdly reverent about an oversized blackberry

no attachment to the land
drunk in its casket

i want you to remember me
like only a fellow cult member can

bills with interest from heaven
another paycheck from hell

postmarked snaking of the mississippi
swallowed by delta

terrified and relentless
yankee transplant competing for truest believer

only by light of day, before the stars start winking
like it's a comedy

but i don't get it, do you?
i assume not, same wolves and all

the only thing i still find funny
is the laughter itself

muffled crying from the dryer
when the hideout becomes blinding

olly olly oxen what the fuck
the game is over, but the door's still locked

if you were raised by the same wolves i was

all that *you'll grow out of it* was bullshit
the tragedies we bawled over as teenagers
are truer now than ever
we are just too tired to keep crying
the anthem of every adult
a heavy resigned sigh
into hazardous ether

gaping at how bad it has to get
before you're doctor-mandated
court-ordered to stop working
and hole up in some underfunded
hospital for the four horsemen
to unearth trembling
in their umbilical armor

mommy vibes monetized
the sense of affection's unsettling
but then again, what else is there
when even an electric current
at the instant of execution
sinks the fingers of criminals
ever deeper into their assassins

inanimate nailed down contraptions
housing rowdy animals
one last time in that polite contortion
upright, flat back, appetites suppressed
pretending this is just the final task
on the to-do list of existence
and then mad science will deflate you

and madder still will trickle in

if you were raised by the same wolves i was

god continues to kill you every day
by tiny bolts of lightning

a jellyfish sting here, sharp pebble there
and oh, look, there goes the yellow

mylar balloon of wasted love
drifting up into the sunset without pause

everyone is a riddle
for the near-miss of fighter missiles through fog

the worst intentions mollified
only by the atmosphere's incompetence

and we run out to swallow the primordial
soup that first formed us

but daddy's lost his sense of humor
a beach town where they don't serve water

blotter paper turned first aid
a bird of prey on every wave

meet me there, you say, but nothing between us
feels the same, not even this, the third dimension

filled with sawdust and abandoned naval bases
not even the unhoped for

neither of us tell in so many words the story
of the state, and if we did

there would be bullets in our loose fangs
and we wouldn't even sound afraid

if you were raised by the same wolves i was

here lie our parents:

sleeping in suspense of disbelief

coked out professors hermetically sealed

box of feelings with the labels ripped off

miraculously unbroken cigarette floating

forgotten in the glove compartment

as mayfly mundane as volcanic catastrophic

in all the pictures, the arm is pulled out of its socket

it took decades to pop back into place

we don't remember how the mechanically intact move

where to hover the hands

to convince them we're human

or is today too late to fool them

on this worldwide ferris wheel reflected in a mud puddle

hotel desk drawer where i redact the bible with ashes

our ancestors deserved better than church

housekeeping will sweep our anonymous last mess

hush-hush under fresh towels, for the next guest

to sniff out   faintest smoke stain, gumshoe hunch

wet snout pressed flush to the ground

if you were raised by the same wolves i was

this, too, is sex:
the river and the whiplash and

the insects stripped of wings
restless excess

rubbish of the flesh
hammered into gems

we don't like to talk about it but
that's how all metals get precious:

indescribable violence
followed by big *oohs* and *aahs*

if you were raised by the same wolves i was

the day the wishing well dehydrates
unto death, so will we
the ultimate hypocrites
spend their whole lives condemning hypocrisy

but then there are the wolves set free
bloodthirst unchecked
slow-motion jugular attack
mounting a banged-up rack of antlers

we wanted to be just like them growing up
strong-armed pups of the apocalypse
picked up by scruff of neck for the village
to spot us stalking fragile outskirts, brush and heather

and gape astonished at the mess
mattes, ticks, and burs hugged close
for the first time, we're embarrassed to be feral
to have known love just enough

to live and no more
for it would spoil us
no more, or else we might learn
we deserve a warmth we can't afford

if you were raised by the same wolves i was

on the fourth of july you buy a bunch of those minia-
ture american flags and burn them one by one over your
kitchen sink, hoping the block party will blow itself up
already. there is no smoke alarm anymore. you knocked it
down with a broom handle for low-battery whining years
ago. merry-go-round of abject inflammation, all by your
lonesome out in the big bad. you were taught how to repair
the world without underwear on, in every polaroid, older
cub, big brother, buried under papers that fail to name
you. the other failure was gender and we laughed the big
dick laugh of girls blown off, rebuffed by the concept of
category. but sometimes we still take them into the base-
ment and huff them until we feel better. tell me: do you
feel better holding that snapshot of me in my bathing suit,
8 years old and writhing like they do in music videos, like
i was raised to do in other people's bedrooms? half light,
half awake, half screaming. flip a coin: there's the devour
half remembered, then there's the rest

if you were raised by the same wolves i was

what's left isn't worth mentioning
a tiny bunker where you sleep sitting up
aerosol poison under pillow, dreaming
a shotgun haunted by honey bees

the last time you got laid in new orleans
he took you out back in the morning
and showed you where the kitchen
transitions into hive, whispering, *they've been here*

as long as i have with an anti-interventionist
gentleness still enviable, estimating the honeycomb
at six feet across behind the siding, scores more hiding
and you imagine whole islands of living upholstery

endangered decorations out year-round
i might be allergic, you say, just to see if his face
can muster feelings past this place, but instead:
a detailed lecture on the extraction of stingers

and for whatever reason, when it's over
you're the one to lock the house, like
there's a prowler on the loose somewhere, like
such a man is any match for what he'd find

if you were raised by the same wolves i was

beware the creatures whose fur smells sugared
charisma memorized as insurance like a backward
alphabet on the blacktop cop cars with their lights on
make me feel like i might seizure and they love it

tonight i don't mind smiling through the jaw dislocation
and saying, *howdy, officer*, as if he isn't the ghettoizing
militia rolled in, tanks idling outside a church's chicken in
atlanta, the dick swing of a generation dotted with rats

escaping shipwreck, or so they hope, but studies show
there is only a 1 in 40 chance of mutating into something
that survives the blitzkrieg licked clean
seas half sick from their own swing

i hide the landfill in my fishnets to reek of what
the world won't want: i'm used to this
the intersection where revulsion meets the hunt
coyote cooing under bedroom window

my only kin this side of dust
unless it's true you were one, too, back then
a pointing mutt under the cedar rot
when scent was all that told apart

if you were raised by the same wolves i was

where we put the fire out, the wet leaves

never rustled out of their rot

the pitter-patter of clawed paws channeling the gods

of mars scarred our stomachs since birth

we nursed from the barrel of a rifle, clicked out a waltz

turning the safety on and off

and it didn't occur to us until today, at long last

music could be made by something else

a ringing in the wind lifted like witchcraft overhead

little echoes of explosions in every pulse i've ever

pressed against: listen long enough and you'll hear it

catchiest melody mumbled from top bunk before sleep

it will tell the story of a flame thrown for nothing

you will learn until it's your burden to teach

if you were raised by the same wolves i was

one of us won't make it out of this city alive, remus

and the other will survive on borrowed posca

missing the ghosts that never bothered to haunt her

what lurks in the forest is none of our business

and yet, that's where myth might have left us

unswaddled little proto-romans dying of exposure

the question is whether the wolves raised us right

who we might have wound up, if petted gentler

but of course there is no answer in the scattering crows

vultures atop mount paladine—how high

do you have to get to believe me? conspiracy

is what they call it when the tongueless start to speak

and the augury of morbid birds still means more

as legend has it, no surrogate parent can protect us

from the onslaught, and when they howled out

our lullabies, they promised no such thing

instead, they said to sharpen our new canines

on the leather of each other

and as sure as rome's still standing

some days i wake still in your teeth

if you were raised by the same wolves i was

what forgotten mammoths
raised them first?

sitting in the rain so long
photosynthesis forgets direction

i wish there were a credit score
for dicks sucked while not in love

i wish i could get rich on all the
drooping tulips in my bloodstream

danger favors zealots
the kind of kids who kick rocks

over the edge of hell
as if there really were a lakeside

as if that's really where we lived
all those years, the kingdom

coming down
as if, on a dare, we jumped in

if you were raised by the same wolves i was

this is no punishment or promised land
only the engine idle of redeye drivers
at the truckstop with your tongue out
only the wave *bye* to the origin
whatever origins are for

if you were raised by the same wolves i was

even the tree line looks concussed

NO TRESPASSING sign with all the warnings ripped off

i deadpan my way through the hyperventilate, but wait

in all the databases my status remains active for taxes

what comes after the scar in the lifecycle of a stabbing?

to disappear completely is a luxury granted only rarely

clouds all cried out, collapsible tantrums

of grown children, metal on metal

we drop trinkets down the house fire

no one can banish us for our recklessness

impossible, we were told

to trespass against ourselves

if you were raised by the same wolves i was

tuning into any shared frequency
takes a village of therapists maneuvering
bunny ears above a television set

when it works, the room falls hush
down to the contraction of lungs
connection is so tenuous, breath breaks things

every day, i look forward to not having any left
letting the dirt defang the past
or sift my pockets for safekeeping from the surface

what i'm saying is i plan on going dormant
still singing loudly at the cellular level
but no longer a threat to the government

there are some hauntings we'd be better off without
but that doesn't stop me from spooning
a ghost every morning

weighing down a bouquet of porcelain
flowers with stones from rome's foundation—
repurpose what pisses you off

in pieces, if needed—
the flood comes in tender cupped handfuls
from someone you didn't know you loved

now that you know, it changes nothing
but the taste of drowning
in their palm

if you were raised by the same wolves i was

a snap in sanity sounds necessary
like rolling down the car window before puking

my uterus is a vessel only for consternation
i yell uselessly into the closed taco bell drive thru

and the vampire bats seem to listen
even several thousand screeches away

from believing in human reason this evening
i still stay inside the traffic lines out of habit

tip my hat to the floodwater, lean into the nausea
they call this city *she* because they swarm the streets

nightly to catch the twinkle in its eye as it's suffocating
jack off accordingly, press their genitalia

like a flower into the page of civilization
and preserve the book for eternity

the library of congress is a ghost to me
rattling the doorknob of inevitable extinction

the world is a shitty sitcom i wish i could fall asleep to
but it's too loud and i'm too late: here comes

the laugh track with no comeback
this is the one where they escape—just wait

if you were raised by the same wolves i was

i'm curious what, if anything, you remember
of being nothing
ball of darkness, the majority of space
a distance between sunspots
slowly expanding the universe far and away
it stays so strange to have a body
when you remember being nothing
as if you aren't entitled to a shape
before birth, before the beginning of the world
you and i, together as nothing
i die, dream, and drug as often as possible
because i remember being nothing
the plasticity between boundaries speaks to me
because i remember being nothing
in fact, i got into philosophy for love of nothing
postulated the nature of consciousness
as if it were exotic
plato regarded all learning, all enlightenment
as an act of remembrance and perhaps he was right
because i remember being nothing
i try to teach it to everyone i meet: how not to exist
how to resist comparing yourself
hilariously against the abyss—
your last gig, which you never officially quit
that place would take you back in a second
and it may sound scary under all that hair and skin
but now that you remember it, it really wasn't that bad
just nothing, after all, just ache unlived

if you were raised by the same wolves i was

let's vacation in freight containers along the lakes like
an eternal shipwreck—i saw that in a movie once, i think
but i'm never sure if i'm talking to you or someone else
anymore, if we were raised the same or differently
together or apart, if this is the cataclysm all wings were
made for or just more lightning calling the thunder's
bluff. the conditional is a constant grown comfortable, its
forked tongue a motorized decoy i'm trying to yell over:

DO OR DO NOT YOU RECALL
THE DAMN WILD DOGS WE CALLED MOM?

still no answer, but i'm convinced despite the silence
we are kin, limp-limbed newborns just yesteryear
a single blanketed pit where we were banished when
bad and the land just keeps shaving its concrete
staying late at the office, mythologizing the punks
we hazed, hair held back by wind, blowing strangers
on the jehovah's witness church lot
they would one day dig for graves

if you were raised by the same wolves i was

speak back to me

in so many strains of disease

focus on the backlit mammary

crags of a mountain half cloud-covered

in the era of sinister chemicals

what happens to sisters ripped

clear of the nursery

a glimpse into the kidnap, the thief

though the official file clearly states

there was no womb   before the wolves

stolen from whom?

a pile of streetwise kicked up with the leaves

oblivion of knives chipping teeth

an intimation of a *lesser evil*

in the jaws of a predator

commingling with the innards of lizards

hoisted by the forces of the forest

up over the cities, with their twinkly

polite little excuses for murder

shitty apologies visible from space

but no, i'm not moving back

                              to the black bear outhouse

last wilderness left

  i'd rather up-in-smoke car wreck while hating everyone

i'd rather turn into someone who doesn't miss

                              what never was

Predators Welcome

the median

we couldn't hold our breaths
the entire tunnel

so you told me your wish:
to be a different person

someone satiable
who knows how best to

scratch the itch of consciousness
well, little wide-eyed panting puppy

i don't know either
but i will dig my fingers

with utmost loving attention
into the skin behind your ears

for a million years
feed you bloodthirsty berries

from the lip of my paltry fountain
whatever doesn't deserve you

i know full well, but i've worked hard
flown all over a dying empire

to tell you to show you
the tragedy isn't lost on me

but i'm enlisting your balled spit
your half-lifted eyelid in orgasm

to write an alternate ending
pass a frantic notebook

back and forth laughing about
the private capacity for violence

in our passing glances over the median
eternally uncrossed between us

steering wheel shaking in both fists
like any moment we might

work up the worst courage
shatter the straight line

and kiss a cursed gear shift
into oncoming headlights

dick is a drug

i'm window shopping for psychoses
feeling so lucky the lightning chose me
almost midnight in the wings of demons
where there was never meant to be an opening
i perched, sipping your snowdrift
a two-toned hummingbird of not enough
whistling a hail mary last letter
before the absence set in, like
FINALLY I AM NOTHING
FINALLY I AM NOTHING
FINALLY I AM NOTHING
FINALLY THE DARK WINS

spirits of long-lost enablers past

this holiday season i'm thankful for my estrangement
a statue of a sad stripper

to compare myself against until i'm dead
the sky was so blank today i mistook it for blindness

the mathematical principle of the cockroach multiplier
at work, i don't understand what straight men are

waiting for; romantic love is vestigial
the future would be lucky to lose it

upgrade the system
to razor-teeth and switchblade acrylics

tiniest touches of evil at the edges of our bodies
rom-com starring our ashes mid-cauldron

pulverize every piece of debris
into something you're proud of

we're here we're queer we're plotting
the end times for the sake of itself

tally up the whole flower like
he loves me trampled, he loves me trashed

he loves me at the bottom of the river
with missing fangs and all the flags half mast

how i want america to end

everywhere we go there is a whisper of a widowing
a soon-to-be-neutered new order
no one else wonders about

touch your leech to mine so tenderly
under this canopy of trees, take nothing too seriously
to wet and wrap around the sores on your hind feet

i igloo into your orbit in your sleep
so you can't tell me *melt*
i wrap my legs around your hellscape

and ricochet like dope about the brain
all wars look weird, no matter where you're sitting
half-soaked in the stadium

even the words for weapons sound antiquated
like we're not supposed to aquarium here anymore
but the ocean's no longer an option either

the question is always just how uncomfortable
you're going to ask me to get for you
a very white shirt on a very red deathbed

is how i want america to end
the way i feel about the fall of empire now is like a
graduation song playing at an execution

so proud to see you reach your full potential by
bending down beneath a reaping scythe
forgetting your own national anthem

stuffing an eagle with runoff chemicals
and calling it the dinner of millions
a country is a strange thing to rage at

so vague in its internal organs but
steel-girt about the borders, flyover fossils
forever documenting which ribs stick out prettiest

and there we are among them, spotted from a fighter
missile, where the more closely we listen
the more the distance, limb from limit

predators welcome

this new year i'm trying that zero-waste lifestyle
where i swallow all the trash

on rare occasion i don't go to bed hungry
i gun you down in every dream

two toxic seabeds of trauma and insecurity
but that's what makes it sexy

breathing the dust of crushed diamonds
like the rich don't matter

when you brag about your recent poker winnings
i say i'd rather burn money than gamble

if you're willing to risk financial ruin
might as well for revolution

come fall asleep deep in the downy fresh snow
in my throat until the pack howls home

how many strangers' faces have i kissed inch by inch
as if rewiring a landmine?

how many lullabies have i invested in the hushing of
bedfellows long dead?

i put up a sign like
PREDATORS WELCOME

pry open the attic windows
left unnailed for this specific purpose

utterly reckless with who i belong to
one sunrise to the next

you could be anyone and yet, the crystal coffin of your
drool-stare down the wreckage

looks comfortable enough to climb into
liquid beginnings of life as we know it, fuck off

i'm trying not to get sentimental for once
about the dried-up erstwhile

pill bug crushed into the office carpet
and preserved there under plastic until spring

we try to crack the prehistoric at the thorax
but we forget: all the worst things have wings

bury me where i was born

on a gravestone back home   *known to god alone*

a whistle in the vinca while all the world roars

we read in old papers the phrase

used for johns and janes left unidentified

plastic bags of hair and bone

where cloudlessness once carried us

behind the motel six on michigan

where the reporters say employees first spotted

the cadaver, something slumped

between the woods and dumpsters

anemone unrecognized

blowup life leaked beyond belief

but i was born across the street, sober begging

to hide under that inscrutable monstrosity

idyllically forgotten, nympho pumped to nothing

bury me illegally, without my given name

atop the bodies of forgotten gods

who alone could know us then?

blushing is just blanketing in blood whatever you want covered up

sometimes the conference call gets dull enough to
fantasize about an active shooter scenario

and we tally all the secret crawl spaces
we could jimmy open with a paper knife

but mostly i wonder what we'd hiss to each other
across the too-hot hallway

we've come to hate, when suddenly enamored
shots fired, chain of command severed

there is only our lungs' muffled heaves
synchronizing into the quietest music

the smell of unexpected flooding
a parish away from the capitol

maybe we would only wordless
doe-eye and click our hooves together

maybe the ten-headed snake in your gut
would go nuclear

substatic upset of two addicts
half hoping for an approaching siren

show me how the song ends mid-stickup
when there is no *after* to overthink

useless to be embarrassed
by all the dying left to do tonight

what security cameras might catch us
crunching between our skeleton teeth

the single cavity carved deep enough
armed men can't reach

my rapist calls to ask for directions

please and thank you for staying

rusted by rainfall

you send me roses the day

after the biopsy like

hands cupped

a second echo chamber

around the mouth's

drowned mischief

darling, all we make

is no difference

with our paper applications

framed paychecks

pleasantries paved over

every corner

another bakery

that lazy waft of day-old

yeast floating up

into the brambles so many

red fangs follow

all in good fun

is what we call predation

until it happens to us

kill the surgeon inside you

scalpel happy

i'm radiant when i get what i want

hornet's nest of fucked up

kicked in its copious cheek

ISO anyone who will egg me on

deeper and deeper into insanity

the language it taught me is what i say

to myself when no one is listening

resigned not to mind the monotony

golgotha after golgotha

mouthing those tired wistful words

not so experienced you're expendable

over and over into the ether

until even i half believe them

dream in which we all tell the truth

my american dream is a torture scene
in ronald mcdonald's basement

o human feats of fortune
eat my freakshow whole

when i descend the staircase fully dressed
i mean: lettuce tomato mayo

when i call my type *scholarly*
i mean of internet pornography

sending ten strips via padded envelope
respectfully collapsing into fairy dust at every

price-matched disappointment, for anyone within
earshot, i'm against all odds hollering your barcode

into the abyss, dialing in just to listen and imagine
living in sin together

but if it's with you, i win   as if the recoil
isn't right around the corner

holding court with whatever air is apparent
between our separate idioms for armor

i swear we called this by a different name once
blow for blow, throat to throat

swollen shut just enough
to tell the truth and hope it guts

stay shelved

so many comrades in recovery
and here i am still mainlining dreams

as if across a crowded room, an angel might articulate
my thought stream worm for worm

face-off too lush to get lost in the figures
ventriloquized incest, tin mood turned to snowmelt

when you use *apophatic* correctly in a sentence
the rest of the world goes mute

and every germ-addled wound is holy
that's what the howling never tells you

explicitly, but it's apparent whole forestfuls of
woodpeckers get it, and we're no different

thank the chaos for deciding to warm itself
on our little spinning bonfire of lead

thank the hospital parking lot for reminding us
childhood has been canceled

since the start and yet it still feels fresh
mazel tov to our mutual collapse

i've been cosmically betrothed to one unmooring or
another for so long wishing it were yours

i've been nine kinds of anemone
the plastic sixer rings skinning their predators

i've been the cliffs where anyone ignoring the weather's
warnings disappears into the drift

but none of that would impress you
the usual terrors stay shelved

pages fingered to the point of crumble
go ahead—i am helpless

to whatever feathers
you next decide to pluck and spread

come to my church

it's just a ditch

at the outskirts of town

where we dare each other

to get murdered

fondle the booby trap lever

with a fingernail sharpened

for sacrificial bloodletting

necromancy isn't dead

shoveled wreaths still litter

liminal spaces with needles

what crowley calls the *all-devourer*

under the snow, hell keeps repeating steam

what if i'm the rogue boneyard

you've been coaxing open

this entire ceremony?

now you see me

in the heist hole

now you're the thief

gunmetal mother

an unimportant loss   is an oxymoron

i'm still fawning over the lone flower staring down

its own reflection in the sunlit side of a dumpster

the image is suspect but   still checks all the

poignant boxes   nothing this delicate lives long

without becoming   the back alley around it

winding its tongue around a carburetor and fellating

what's tomorrow   scrapped for parts

patron of the arts   say you'll subsidize

the exploratory surgeries that pacemake my forgotten

frame into an origami   starfish of not giving a fuck

a tax-deductible one-off   to write home about

and then cast backhanded into the quarry

no one is sorry   for all the roses left rotting

and why should they be?   there is only so much to see

before the whole world goes   gunmetal mother

harpooned cartography   that once-a-jungle green

afraid to say

getting murdered is the ultimate party entrance

you thought i was going to say

exit, but that's too obvious

most wars are waged over this precise difference

whether the choke-out is a drug that

actually takes you someplace, or just deposits you—

fat jug, crushed balloon—no such paradise of pink

the problem is   no one has gotten over anything

the afterlife is only a movie where we pretend

we can move on   but where to?

the hole is empty   by definition

perfection is a picture of a cross-country runner

shooting himself in the foot over and over on loop

by the time we descend the snow-coated ladder

it's whatever, we could limp from here—

the weather's fake

but let me tell you, there are insects

deep underground right now

who know what's coming

and they're afraid to say

only decent party in light years

everybody says they are ready
for the questionnaire, but can they really

trace the filament holding together
rapid cycles of internal weather? never

i don't deny them the underbelly of the mountain
the pure pleasure of the heart starving over and over

most of the multiverse is numb, to be sure
so wherever there is red-hot capacity

latch fast the door   gather everything electric
convince yourself it's worth the burns

to radiate the stink unbuttoned
more and more with each emerge

to be seen is to be consumed

everything is creepy up close
when i open the office
watch the heater shake loose

no one is coming to save us
daddy's dead as dust
shroud of tourists, candied metaphysic

pointless beauty
halved by computer monitors
wave hi to me

through the interrogation glass
this mirror might not be
as two-way as it seems

following the north star home

outside the gallery   i liquidate

my personality down to absolute shock factor

like how a week before   i proved myself   hymenless

my mother said   *get fucked*

fomenting like she almost meant it

i'm through grooming   prosthetic humans

instead i stare down stonehenge in spare moments

smoke a blunt over my lunch break

make a donation to the church of *ouch*

whatever disease i caught from the cathedral rafters

the desert can't cure   the fertile lurch   poised crouch

what came before   this hind-leg rigmarole

bored meetings bent to fit   behind an asterisk of shit

all the pigeons and penthouses   eye-level with

the end of their species   happy sendoff

soldier standing silhouetted by the sunset   machine-

gunned meat   begets machine-gunned meat

that's what mom must have understood

when she said that   tree rings and bullet casings

only know how to accumulate   and woven into

the walls of their nests   there we writhe

tic-tac-toeing oblivion   in the jumpsuit of a suicidal

prisoner and for good reason   take a lesson

from who else lives between   loose slabs of plaster

pitter patter of rats   confused owl trapped in the attic

i'm ecstatic in the parking lot   to ditch this half-baked

art scene and booty call the north star   but no

no one's seen him since last fall

when there was a council on who   could or couldn't

follow him home   and he decided

like they all do   he was better off alone

for lack of posterity

face of predation the only constant across landscapes

if it doesn't break the skin, did we even make contact?

at all hours of nightlife, who do we name

new stars after? a killer and

a willing victim

opening its breastbone for the squall to trickle in

photoshopping the breakup

i am leaving you
everywhere i go
like dna evidence

sorely unmissed
loose strands
blown to bits

if the forgetting
were this easy
would you ever

flinch to fall
head over heartstem
into grim wist

i hack up my hecklers
every night before bed
even a sin-eater

would get sick to her stomach
on this bilious river
turning mucosal ocean

we don't dare recognize
the residue of friends
on a stranger's shoulder

clean breaks are photoshopped
for press releases
i wrote myself

subtextual loss

the art may not be hard to master
but there is still a learning curve
for table manners at the banquet
of personal disaster

and where is everybody
from before, i wonder?
don't tell me
don't tell me

i'll be able to guess
by the end of the episode
i'll shave my head and listen extra close
for the *no* under the universe's breath

goodbye would be a lie

reading over my seatmate's shoulder   exitless
greyhound bus to adulthood

the experience of being eaten   present-tense
intraocular blizzard

transmission sent by pigeon   *forget me*
but who could possibly

the wolf is waiting   last stop
chicago tarmac

all the people raise their hands   as if to worship
distance

at its rawest thickness   but what about it
when where i come from

cleaves to the lynching scene
goodbye would be   a lie so i   just leave

how best to fall

there are always sparrows flying through this airport
what showoffs   to need no machinery
naked as glass   fresh blown
it feels best to be touched places people could kill you
throat, flank, thigh   insides in the night
i caught the *my best friend is dead* disease
and now   and now what
when we can't undress to find out
none of the multiple altar calls at your funeral
saved anyone   except the memory
of hellfire reflected in your sunglasses
so i ditch the service to piss in a ditch outside
plaid skirt hiked waist-high, broad daylight
bracing myself against the back of the brick edifice
someone so carefully selected for your final defilement
but, baby   i would have buried you in drag
birth name struck down   conversion journals burned
if i only had the clout   of cartoon deities on clouds
i'd weave whole solar systems into your hair extensions
scavenge the gates of heaven for raw jewelry metals
sin is a fiction we've both been to rehab for
and i'm sick of explaining its track marks to the masses
packaging our church trauma
into clever digestible morsels of crisis
i lift my hands amidst the congregation
but not the way they want
to fly our freak flag over all
to respond to this   anonymous pastor

i am finished decoding kindness for a plague of locusts
with painted doorpost   i'll pass over the cornfields
stealing nothing   taught by the sky how best to fall

Acknowledgments

I would like to thank my sister, wolves everywhere, and all the early readers and audiences of these poems, especially John Barrios, Christopher Payne, Caitlin Simmons, Garret Strickland, and Elias Gwinn. I'd also like to thank Kimberly Sheridan Owen, Lisa-Marie Basile and Cameron Lovejoy for featuring the following selections from this book in their respective journals:

Abandon Journal: "autopsy reveals lasting marriages mostly composed of sharp metal in a theoretical vacuum"

Luna Luna Magazine: "the median" and "stay shelved"

Tilted House Review: "how i want america to end," "spirits of long-lost enablers past," and "predators welcome"

Author Bio

Dylan Krieger is writing the apocalypse in real time in south Louisiana. She is the Managing Editor of *Fine Print* and the author of six earlier collections of poetry: *Giving Godhead* (Delete, 2017), *Dreamland Trash* (St. Julian, 2018), *No Ledge Left to Love* (Ping Pong, 2018), *The Mother Wart* (Vegetarian Alcoholic, 2019), *Metamortuary* (Nine Mile, 2020), and *Soft-Focus Slaughterhouse* (11:11, 2021). Find her at DylanKrieger.com.

1

LIMIT ZERO
PUBLICATIONS

Milton Keynes UK
Ingram Content Group UK Ltd.
UKHW021216100324
439016UK00007B/101

9 781938 753480